11. 95

HURRIYA

HURRIYA

poems by

Steve Noyes

TSAR
Toronto
Oxford
1996

The publishers acknowledge generous assistance
from the Ontario Arts Council and the Canada Council.

Cover Art:
War in Kuwait, 1992, wall work construction in relief, centre detail
(92 cm x 120 cm), by john m Orser. From his continuing program of
artwork LIFE DURING WAR TIME. Image used by permission of the
artist and Visual Arts Studio, 6081 Old West Saanich Road, Victoria, BC,
V8X 3X3.
    The painting *War in Kuwait* directly addresses the reality of war in
the era of technology. A war on the environment, and the very basis of
our human ecology are sustaining and continuing. The fundamental
impact of this war is on our thinking, forcing humanity to conform to
the realities of technological warfare as a reasonable and normal
human proposition. War, its technology and thinking becomes accepted
as part of the human identity, it precludes other realities and states of
being.   Om Mani Padme Hung
                john m Orser

Canadian Cataloguing in Publication Data

Noyes, Steve
    Hurriya : poems

ISBN 0-920661-61-0

I. Title.

PS8577.096H8 1996   C811'54   C96-932073-6
PR9199.3.N69H8 1996

TSAR Publications
P.O. Box 6996, Station A
Toronto, M5W 1X7 Canada

For Susan Gillis,
articulate companion

Contents

1. Believable Motion

2. Koy

3. :omar

4. Hurriya

1. Believable Motion

AFTER THE SIXTIES

These our wanderers
awent from home in rain
Holding to land in rain
in every wall-wormed city they became
known of the road and wearier
than words for newspapers
And none remembered time
"It's funny," one was heard to say
"Ever since twenty I don't have any
sense of it, of what my age is ."
"Why that's like me," another answered
and their hands were warm
in the light of their fire on stone
which was everywhere with
as they went on
Sometimes in grey distance
caravans they sighted spanned
a day of walking and a night
and day again
"Look," one said, and look
the far edge of the world
was narwhal   centaur   wind
Or saw spaced flowers of fire
and smoke afar and stopped
afraid to say anything

No one had brought a radio
but now and then they noticed spring
in swarming insects or their own
increasing pace and were no longer nervous
"That was spring, remember?"
"Where was that place we were?"
"What place was that?"
There was surprise once on a valley
food had been a constant problem
and they had eaten
looking at the valley and the rain

3

fall was of temple bells
and vertical skulls.

THE INTERIOR

And on we are the highway
which idea is from the Skeena
we flow beside can get
there because the river's
grey-green eating of distance
full of miles and not
lost
silly a river's never lost and finds
force in itself and variables
of grey gun fishflesh green
a way back to its name along
a course in pebbles here
and bankbite there
little by little but never showing
takes back the highway
narrow
shaken by trucks
The city's easier
to talk about unless we think
entirely in rock and tree
sky and scenery
roadside weeds in bloom no names for
the feeling it's possible still
to think while moving

*

If none move through it
through the land with money

and time to spend
the small towns die
puzzled cells with no clear
course or organized identity
reverting to what's only necessary
food and fuel and tools
wood into money
in this way poised
between a shrill vibration
and ominous stillness
(are you still with me
says the Skeena)
store signs with absurd spellings
groping for the lost code
each cell lives longer and longer into its own death
becomes utterly like itself
in high smoke over forest

*

For each person a meaning
or the land matches something in each
who want a meaning
the clear-cut slopes
ledgers and pencils
a twenty grand summer
where a boy can be a man
for five months and a boy
for twelve months and the year
goes in the bank
dead fallers
drunk whistlepunks and crafty scalers
the names are free and clear

And the boys trot to the theatre
sit one seat apart
with no girl between them
who lives on a poster
on the foreman's wall

5

Take good care of yourself
you belong to me
she whispers
to all of them in particular
not there and there
in her adorable sweater
the empty seat

*

The lovers held
arms to keep

from sliding on steep gravel
and picked at the skeleton
a woman sitting
as though stopped for a picnic
with someone else's bones
where her lap was
and ashes for hands
cartridge in her skull
the lovers
afraid of falling and curious

the inside and the outside
of their bodies

*

The airport town fogged in
slow music of the mall
breaking in siren for an Indian
man has fallen
banged his head
and seems not to know his name
so the bystanders the whole ring
of waiters and watchers
get asked by attendants
What happened?

Do you know who he is?
Some people walk off.
I don't know.
Yeah, he's an Indian.
You mean his name?
Anyway he is taken care of
and the crowd relaxes
There is a man
slung with guns and fishing rods
on the phone not relaxing.
I can't get out tonight.
I love you too.
Shit, I'm in a place called . . .

"I WAS CERTAINLY LOST"

Those who travelled years
at the edge of a sere
heat—where exactly varied—
say something appeared
in the punishing air. It
was built long ago
and still in motion.
Moon-wide wheels
begun in cloud
stole substance as they turned
and strove. Long levers
of the thinnest, flexing bone
engaged and moved the wheels below
while the faces of those known
revolved with green-gold,
rough stone. Fresh vines,
flowers trailed—or did they—
from the smooth arcs so

when visitors returned
they mentioned "towering gardens"
—as if they could not see
the wheels at all;
though some men
made attempts to shape
in listeners' minds
a soundless constancy,
precision of grip
with which the huge gears
glided and the senses
(smell of dust)
(glints within)
were renewed: old loves
urgent children;
repetition so fresh
some likened it to hands
pouring cool water
during illness
or the time
locked in embraces.
But men fell silent
after such efforts
drew away with smiles
playing on their faces
now and then, content.
They could no longer want
to say what pulsed
behind their eyes. Such men
seemed filled, grew
twilit. Occasional
grimaces and gestures
(for few stopped trying
completely to explain)
were more uncalled for:
like swirls of wind
just outside the village
stinging the eyes
or thin dogs slipping

around a tent
and gone.
Still men discussed
the vague machine
over their drinks
at night—the splendour,
its possible applications
—and ended arguing stupidly
about their businesses.
The records indicate
no organized attempt
to find the ornate ghost
(no maps exist).
The very best account
this, of a dying merchant:
"I was certainly lost, with no hope,
and sank to my knees and prayed
only to find myself standing and, oddly,
sinking. I felt sand
scraping my belly then
my eyes, when I saw
with a new and trembling strength
a chain of turning discs
from the sky to the earth. Discs.
I mean they were huge—waterwheels?—
they weren't waterwheels. They had no
spokes, no gourds, but vast
medallions that spun and
slowly spun so I was lifted—
you doubt. From far above
(for I rose, I rose) each edge
was intricately tiled. I hovered
there: each wheel sank past me.
I saw—well, it wasn't clear
if they were there before or had just appeared
and I grow tired. There were
people—but not-people—quaking, sick.
Their ribs, their bony haunches.
Crawling on those paths that rimmed

the wheels, being borne downwards,
curving as off the world. And then
the same wretched bodies
came into being, on each lower wheel.
Some of them clutched the loose skin
on the necks of small white bulls . . .
I do not know what they wailed . . .
Spears and jewelry, coins, fell
from the structure, but I didn't
see or hear them land—as the ill
revolved, ever lower. Standing in midair
a long moment, I had such a thought—
a crazy thought. Then calm. It was
the beautiful intactness, the whole motion,
circling and sinking. Oh yes, an inexplicable
hint of smoke. I cannot tell you the thought
I had; I cannot tell you much.
The moving limbs, the linked
eternity—I rant. But then
I spoke these words:
Desire resumes the earth.
Then I had weight in my legs,
saw only the heat flexing
above the sand and I turned
around, thinking only of the way here.
Certain of it."

BLOOD

One fall was restless
to see—passed
the vast stadium where runty
Mack Herron had zig-
sped bearing earth
coloured ball to get
busted for coke
and the convert net sagged
given up waiting
—to see Grandma and Grandpa
who'd given up too
but never on waiting

They both shook my hand
in the rude-smelling kitchen
crisp shirt and suspenders
boxy old frock
in the rude-smelling kitchen
we ate mouldering stew
they remarked on my blue
pants and jacket
When had I joined the navy?
Refusing more stew
  it was fine
  I was full
in their faces I knew
I was learning to lie

And they sat there not speaking
by habit not laughing
or crying in public or private
     a relic
of marriage you mouthed once
and stuck to
  so I told them
of blue mist and harbours
my Rangoon tattoo

neither held with that practice and Grandma
snapped back to her room

Hoe for a cane
he led me to his garden
we enjoyed burning leaves
he chopped a cat's head off
and told me again the damn priests
started wars
              lost his leg
                      were to blame
he better not catch one in his yard
Inside the house
Grandma thought out loud about singing
Standing still in the leaf smoke
I glared at the church with him
at the crisp cold on the coloured glass
having my first doubts about things
especially the navy

SALISBURY PLAIN

The flatness of it. The calm
and calm's interior regret at no
uphill or agitation, no strain still
against a pressure, pull. The land extends.
The rivers fingers of an idle hand.
Above the earth the sun, the stars, the sun
and mist around the here and there black trees:
all grittily gone to air when done
with thinking of it ten thousand years ago.
The walking humans did, the to, the fro.
Compact, stunted one would say, their speech
unknown, my ancestors, walking and talking
like apes lug sticks across the plain,

water in mud-wide baskets, any animal
made draggable. They make for home.
The wood is lit and centre becomes fire.
They sit and stir.

And there were grunts of names, knees
prodding against thighs, a rising
highness to the odd voice, cries
scraping the dirt, the snap
of branches in the fire. An opening
of legs to urgent hands the only channel
down which I stare; their love more visible
to others caught in bones around my eyes.

(Silence. The low worship of each other. The vast dark.)

There's little else. My father left the plain,
his father dead, a young man near this century's beginning.
Walked upright to the train station, where he could hear
the low throat of his going some ways off.
The family house was stone, had held the delicacy
of curtains to the light. He looked back
and was gone.
                    Since you asked
about the past, I'd say to know
this little is itself desire, will do.
What else is home?

COUNTRIES

In my country
there are many people talking
loudly talking of not being
where they are in bar or living room
not being comfortable or warm with drink
in belly beautiful and young nor
having the money of our country
ready on the table
to never tip the comely help
and they talk about themselves
—how things were west or east
of red soil on the island and the roads
rife with potatoes
of the fiery chains of maple leaves
through which grey farms
appear to die at home in old Ontario
or miles in their eyes of prairie

And something in me responds
which has no bearings
being a flare of nerve ends nightly
starfish in the streetlights once I
holding a wheel in Halifax around a curve came
wide awake on course in wet Vancouver
such are the distances contained
in what they speak of:

The young people are unemployed
miserably happy
as if no use has used them well
and set them squarely before court and mercy
the weekdays and the joy
of aimless envy
Things are better in Alberta they say
and certainly Toronto why a buddy
made a bundle back there or
America—

But they do not go there
that densely connected empire
whose city lights touch
on the highways and whose secret
riches underneath a mason's apron lie
They fume instead in thrall
to Lords of Winnipeg Regina
cold arms of jewels outside which
fires burn in blackness
sentinels of snowfall
                    Why
it seems for such an isolated pity
of themselves their utter helplessness
—anything could take them
—promise of or promise broken
—as airwaves are shot through
by southern signals—nothing
can be made or fashioned

The young mime this or that subjection
and the land outside the wondering mind
arranges only into emblem
                    "the country of our defeat"
My friends sit powerless
dreaming is it not passing brave to be employed
and ride on credit through Metropolis?

But I can't think that not
of Mary-Ann wiping off tables in New Brunswick
or Michael in the K-Mart on the Island
and can't help smiling
whoever the king is is by some well served
though talk troops dark through that dominion
and even kings cannot hold back the ocean
and service of the many made as snow
blankets for babies' breath can come
together and tongue yes from no
—In meantime term me a temporal fugitive
who sits amidst these hands and heads

and of wet wood and of glass and of the glow
of beer's pronouncing yellow
make a country.

WESTCHILDE

After years of ease in lotus land, you know, I drove
Off a ferry into the prairie through the darkness.
Say: He was seeking constellations,
Lucubrations, speed,
Adrenaline. At three a.m.
Even my wrought-up elbows loved the corrupt
Socreds for their Coquihalla,
The amortized, stellar lanes, and loved
New moon through the sunroof.

Animal off the median near Merrit.
Clouds brightened,
High mountain road, flurries without warning
Signage in my highbeams.

Fuzzbuster busted useless in the glovebox,
What good's it in the glovebox, but the fuzz
Were elsewhere questioning their never-never danish
Deeds away from my blue four-cylinder.
                                        Easy,
Mister.
        Sucky-sweet refills,
                        The first trucks, loggers,
Young man squatting on his lunchbox,
    Millsmell putrid in my nostrils.

Strange way to leave the body,
Strange way to travel, rock and air and eye and water.

16

Strange way to see oneself: spectre
Of the windy mirror.

(Who is to match you for wandering and nightmare,
Amid the terrors of a traveller, the banshee's fetter.)

*

Winnipeg was infernal, medieval host of flood and dust and insect,
North Main stinking in its languages, its golden domes in elms, its
    newspapers and markets.
Summer in the radio, asphalt in cyrillic characters,
Boys in cut-offs, girls in halters,
The short-sleeved ties of Middle Europe, Ukrainian-Cree
Cheekbones.
Zenith.

O its multipurpose parks and sidewalks,
O its deathly veterans,
O its killing floors and red abuses,
O beat policemen in their winter robes
Of buffalo

O Red River.

Runn'st thou far enough to knowe
A roote is a diaspora
What flow'st ironlike
Through thy youth thou lov'st
Effluvia.

*

But I overrun. The wind
A long ways off, Saskatchewan. A little progress.
Another dawn.
                Mosquito ditches.
Calgary moon.
                Trees abandon

17

Combine rows,
    Surrounded houses.
                    Magpie.
Rape and mustard.
    Lilt and sight and scent.
Far-off.
            I been talking to grease monkeys

I had forgotten that.
                    Salt-lick surface.
Mica-hatted silos.
                    Billboards proclaim Christ,
the Blackfoot nation labour pool,

        Wire and thyme.

I been hanging round grain elevators

                    Swaling green the creeks
the gulches.
            Boxcars named for northern states, for oceans,
grain of ascension.

                    Two-lane near Gull Lake,
The sun.
            Planet of the canopy,
                        hanging.

Retina, morning to my Black Cats and romantic blue,
Redhead and a butterfly net waved at you
My old four-cylinder.
            I been talking with hitchhikers.
                    500 clicks to Winnipeg.
            Helium factory.
                    Drink-derrick, drink-derrick,
                    There's a thirsty bird
            Red Deer, Talasata, Medicine Hat

                    Springing swinging antelope.

18

The lake of isn't black wet on the road crown.
  Swallowloop,

Flat, they say.

            Expansive.

*

Of course who wants to read about nature and the prairie,
what-I-did-on-my-summer-holidays:
Back to Main Street: way back when we had a parade
From the Disraeli Bridge to Main and Portage.
There were Oldsmobiles and ragtop Caddies,
Go-go girls and clowns and hippies,
One little two little tom-tom boom and phony headdress
Quaking down the Main.
Past the Occidental and the Native Friendship Centre,
The Museum of Man and Nature and Birt's Saddlery and Leather,
The motorcade slowed and wagonbanded underneath
        James Richardson and Sons'
Megamouths made speeches in the scraper's shadow.
Miss Folklorama was enchanted by a rockstar singer,
And he wore bells and silk
She her Suzy Creamcheese and Cowichan sweater,
And the young men tossed their hair in hunger.
One celebrant received an outsized cheque of styrofoam,
An impossibly curved hockey stick,
A bright Jets sweater.

The whirlpool ache and liniment
And what goes after—
Memory and alcohol.
Slowly the Zamboni surfacing the glare:
His image on a pin-up poster,
Tower of blackened muscle, exultant, with his brothers.
Haybales, pitchforks and the sun's sad glory

On his back. He won for us. We paid him well,
His meat, his strength. The women
He expended in and battered.

I've known parades invariably to
Snake their other in them,
Slough and shine, shine and slough,
Succession.

*

Westchilde, pussycat,
where have you been?
We took the Corydon-Kenaston
To visit the Queen.
Where did the trolley slip?
Redwood and Main.
Where did the drunk sit?
Beside us. It rained.
What did he say?
He told me one day
There won't be a Queen.

What did he mean?

I saw them! I saw them!
Who did you see?
Elizabeth. Philip.
He talked with a hippy.
What did he say?
What are you doing,
young man? My father's fedora
smelled damp and ungainly.
I am fighting for peace,
And just hanging out.
Philip was pleased.
Elizabeth sneezed.
My mother went Bless you.
Westchilde where were you?

Pussy, do tell.
Main Street and Broadway,
Across from the Railway,
The Fort Garry Hotel.

*

So match me catastrophic who remembers
Main Street after Penny Lane,
Threnody of empire. I'll have you know
I visited my Grandfather.
And he didn't recognize me!
Had to tell him. Grandson, is that a fact,
Heh, heh. Deer Lodge kept him busy.
What did I think of the doilies he made?
It's not too bad here. Ashtray I'm making.
Food's lousy.
A plastic leg, a nylon daff, a metal deer outside his window.
Hast thou known a ghost ache in the whirlpool vanished?
The mustard's anger?

On Cordite Road the viscid armatures
Sink in the cess.
          Black pool of bolts.
                    Dragonflies empalanquin.
O isn't in their wingbright music, distant, something missing?

Suburban pipes and kilts, the velvet banners
Skirling in the mind's fear of recurrence,
So many dead, so many maimed,
So many to remember.
The amassing clans.
Come when summer's over.

You know I went to see my father,
That suspicious Englishman
Who knows me least but at least knows me.
Lost in a comfortable apartment
And what comes after—

And he scrutinized me. Some
Judgment he was making.
He read, kept busy, what did I think of astral travelling?
Your mother had a stroke.
Oh, for God's sake, I'm okay.
A tiered parkade, a thunderbird, a satellite dish outside their window.
The astral journeys I've had lately.

Ah, Saint Vital and the Seine's thick grasses,
My parents tired in my eyes, had to lie down, and I left,
Left Winnipeg, the sugarbeet outskirts and the driving dirt,
My neighbours watering their roofs of incubi.

So families turn from families awander,
Always have,
Perchance we may know ourselves a little,
The constellations.

The febrile deer sleeping in the heavy nets,
So tranquil,
That came upon them from a helicopter.
Shit-smeared legs.
                            Cricket pavilion.
Venus.
            Boys in Case caps steered a beater to the shoulder,
Left it for dead.
            My breath again

And what comes after—

So match me in my prayer:
Westchilde, westchilde, tell me the news,
Your mother is tired and your father confused,
The cat and the fiddle, centennial spoon,
Your people were used,
Fluoride and smallpox, asbestos and glue,

The banshee's fetter.

The oxcarts, sacks of flour and breakfast cereal,
Pigtails and scrubbed faces painted
On the city's bricks

O Red River

2. Koy

The chronotype—as explained by an Isma'ili woman interested in such things—may be as small as a hand gesture or eye makeup, as large as a mosque or mall; it is the imprint of a specific culture absorbed in an instant, and can involve all the senses. For the traveller, especially the unsophisticated one, there is the added illusion of temporal vertigo. Since cultures have evolved forward from the past (or since this is the most common way we are equipped to see this process), what the tourist sees (prepared often to only see the quaint, the historical) of the "other" seems powerfully old and undiluted.

As if any culture were pure or uninfluenced. To travel unaware of the accelerated effects of the twentieth century is to be overwhelmed by cheap juxtapositions.

This is by way of introduction to this series of poems, composed during and after a stay in Turkey in the late eighties. For me it was an introduction to Islam, but also to the sense that God is one and humanity is one.

But what is typical about human experience? Mores and customs vary widely across neighborhoods, across class boundaries . . . one might well be in two or three different cultures in the same Canadian city within two or three miles, or two or three flights of stairs.

So, with an initial salute to Edward Said, whose book *Orientalism* first alerted me to the limitations of certain ways of looking at Muslim culture, I suppose all I can do is offer these poems as artifacts of a stage of my own ignorance. My encounter with "the other" has taught me that the words *Muslim* and *Turk* are about as useful labels for human beings as *Canadian* and *Christian*. And yet there was a certain enchantment for me in being in this predominantly Muslim country; if the spell was one composed of naivete and ignorance, let me just say that while ignorance is certainly not bliss, naivete may be, for a while.

PALIMPSEST

Adore, the Sultan in a depth of bent rags
jewels, slaves
The hammered sense of the orient, into us.
Crushed coriander, diplomatic gold
He breathes the cruelty of his nose
Till bored of it, new games
The eunuchs prod sick janissaries forward
into orderly arrangments, chess
to be killed. The tiles and carpets of a time.

Court the concoction.
The twins stand up and whirl, lop lo and each beheads
Look on, God's shadow needs a hookah
Water rills away neat cut-ceiling stars
The tiles, no one remembers how to glaze
The blue between the robes and beards, none other
Kalabalik!   crowded

Rent
the grey in the blue
Marmara rain
And ordinary hats about their business
Overhead walkway, morning rush, Sirkeci station
The followed and some of the following—

IRMAK   river

Eventually one tires of the littoral,
the stony Med, stark and the blue.
The fabled pirate Salman Riis, cowled from the
sea, facing the towns
must too, tire.
Ah, what of the riparian Turk

the river glint through orchards
glowing off and on through years, a certain
span, olive what God hath wrought, dwellings
stoned in the colour of
Do not be sorry, it is a life.
Seen through enchantment, the flash of clear water
running on, running glorious, *guzel irmak*   beautiful river
growing old in the birdsong, in the same
layers of clothes, woodpile to dungpile
a lovable trundle, the needs of goats and familiar
tasks . . .

The sea glitters under the streak, roar
air space
Jets stretch and peg, tighten, in you, map.
Greece, NATO, unavoidable.
Bristle, outpost, these our hills
How to speak other than the
Hard billboard, *Remember Cyprus,* and the river,
and all your labours running under in silence . . .

TUGRA

calligraphic seal of a Sultan

The layering initial of the name,
the interval of script, bellish,
elonga, labora, develops
in different colours on the screen,
Topkapi Palace, no, Musesi Islami
Istanbul, coffee boys
and their fastidious English, you
will like loukum.   Turkish delight

        On screen
the magnificent, the great the seal
whatever, how a line is drawn
in time, imprinted, fixes,
ramifies, tree of belief. The name's
fantastic rigging, ship's, no face
to be seen. Ampersand or clef
that we sailed forth
established this conquered that
set these men with their beads clicking
among it, to warm themselves.

The script, its cursive
limit, sight to speech, of only
loving the loops and flourishes, unknowing
alphabet the eye, stops and, starts
what breath is between, what quality.
As the reversely unversed might love "flourish."

Run of gold inlays in
hanging banners are not piteous, the wringing
eyes of saints, but God exactly written
hard, into the world, a heaven in
which we, easy with the hauling throat and
glassy rasp speak Arabic: an erasing was
lines maddened forward and back, erasing same,
the said, identity mistaken.
The words hang on the palaces, vines.

29

KURD

This my friend is a most difficult word.
This word it is official non-existent.
Where did you hear it?
A sly word this and many people who
have not the reality use, see
some uncle tromping over a hill.
Is interesting, you heard it?
Please sit and we will talk a little. Many think
is a blood around in them, and arrogant, and
what? Pressure hoses? Testicles?
It is not that, my friend, we know intentions.
You see its flagrant K on underparts of bridges?
Cost citizens!
Are using them to work in the Republic
much money to remove.
Such activities in time may weaken the bridges.
Yes, it is nice to chat like this.
Dirty and lazy men who are not modern,
ruin your holiday, snow is very very deep.
Eat from their hands on filthy mats.
They want everyone to know
Is like they offer their daughters to tourists.
No, we read the papers, we say what we think
in Istanbul squares.
But I think you have not been here long.
You must be careful
you are using these words.

THE BARBER OF BODRUM

The youngest son begins to shave him;
stands barefoot on hair and dry soap
behaving, blade on a
bony American throat. And slender
between these he shaves with short
strokes. And we're all a bit nervous.
The shaven clears his thoughts to fix on
Resdan, Barbican, any damn bottle
with "an" on it, on the distant
counter of a motel mirror, and the calm
has a quality, the corner of a postcard.

With firmness the father says, *Ah, you have*
BIG *dollar. Tea?* Suppose you grow up.
You will and you will say what you want.
Like *Brylcreem,* one *patlican, rajul* want *razor.*   eggplant/ man
Glass in the sink may, or any red thirst may
awaken your friend. He will gulp and grow up
any time now. By the time man and camels
along the white wall, the green leaves and tangerines
pass from the mirror, the boy will be finished
his throat.
                Inshallah, inshallah,
boy and God willing.

31

BALID

He stood in his boy jacket in the doorway shrugging his shoulders.
In the doorway where he slept nights with or without the heater,
depending on the tourists' needs, he shrugged.
And turned away, glum, his small back to the street.
Sat on his bed his jacket done up near the safe.
Where he had to say no, I don't go to school, I am ten, and watched his
older
cousins kicking the ball, hands in his jacket, where he saw the old man
approaching, he watched, and turned.

Because he was ten and the booted ball sped directly for the old man.
He turned, and went in near the phone, because it hit.
Because his cousin's pet monkey and electronic keyboard and school,
he shrugged in his jacket, hit in the back, the man whirled, Balid
turned.
His cousins stifling their grins, and went in.
Ten years old, his small back, his jacket done up, the man shaking with
anger, Balid turned from the door and went in.

EVET   yes

A very long aid is available, not curt.
In a wood-tile game
The hand hovers above and satisfied
Clicks.
Twice naming that chatter to press
Warm steam against glass.
My it's hot, think I'll put on another toque.
Do not be too quick to agree; let your lungs aim it
Steadily, a stream to the teeth:
They'll take it.
I like my tea to sound like unspinning sugar
That clings till the spoon's still.
The sentimental song can glide and afford to for a lilt
is forthcoming and the eyes never closed.

RENKLER   colours

You think each colour is a country?
Hue you would stand up in a stadium and recognize?
Column it so, the blueblack tunics of the children
School-air lifting from their lips, anthem.

What background portrays the civic legend
To advantage of his best peaked fingers, ruminative,
Or his eyebrows. Well? Green a fading
Hardware catalogue, a liniment, the smoke lifting level
For a silent annual minute.   to commemorate the
                                             death of Ataturk

A most sleek aubergine
slams in the

33

slams in the rock
against octopus.

Oiled bark-brown of a rifle, beams in the house
Of evening, brown of a beetle's serrated claw, of a dusty
Fiddle screech and the urchin's professional wail

Ayaaa Halima you're so cruel

And he not old enough to really know this knows it
Utterly, so practised yet in singing it the song scabs
In him; when he meets the women's eyes it is another
Rusty panel he can unfasten, lean against the house

Of evening.

Blue eyes everywhere in the market, talismans.

Red gold in the male faces making crowd,
Confusion of small brass colours which are
Century-old weights, and passersby
Nutshells cluttering a wheelable cart, its bulb . . .

Night where the gravel is its crunch purely . . .
Unappealing black and grey pipe frames
Where the market was

But isn't, now

You must say, excuse me, the sky it is *painted* black
It is our language.

MEALS OF THE EARLY REPUBLIC

1.
Odd, that dusk squares out the rotted beams,
Dusts the fezzes, and the hooked, curvaceous pipes
Hold flame-coppers.
Shadows make and wreak, leaping,
The smells in walls.

Meals of the Early Republic.
And the men smoke robed in their corners.
Breathing out ghostly Os afloat
Aflear off the plates. The wind
Gathers outside, us together.

Who is he that drags along the wall, hating
You he sees through
Uncles, brothers, drags, a sack
Of kin, honour, opinon.
He drags it outside, leaves what you make of him.

Your eyes staying open.
A shout across the snow today for tembele Ali   lazy
And the villagers shouting back:
Why call on yourself?
No, I am shuja: Ali!   brave
Not over here.

Your eyes, staying open.
Your meal is late, a smell
The others dream, it comes

To you, the changing.

2.
Early Meals of the Republic, before the ubiquitous
Posters of the Gazi, who in another   holy warrior
Frozen city writes long, long diplomatic letters in French
Living out of a train station, living out of an agricultural school,

Living for braziers, getting sarcastic replies
From the British: "What happy news!
So your people now abjure their cruelty?"
Halide enters, she means business.

A life for argument.
A life for Halide's corrections.
A life for a telegraph.
Cumhuriyet.

The Gazi stays up, and up.
"I want to sleep but I cannot sleep."
The lamplight mutters to itself about air.
And her, "Is that a threat, Pasha?"
Probes, stings.
The telegraphs are singing in, the light is dull,
reports, more threats—
Bring raki.

3.
Meals of the Early Republic.
Pasha X whirls in snow.
His kalpak white, that particles eat
Defends the border unimportant.
He is wounded near the unimportant border.
Muhammad said stay near the mountain
But they followed him, mistake.
From the Qur'an he latterly sang
That all on the earth would vanish.

Heavy walled.
Erzerum, Eskishehir, the boots shone,
The cleave of coats.
The faces tensed at hooves.
Coalsmoke.
Mountain, clear of men.

Halide Edibye, writer,
feminist, one of the
founders of modern Turkey

republic

licorice-flavoured
alcohol

fur hat

Battle of Badr

two cities in
Anatolia

4.
Finally, Isha call to prayer   last prayer of
Is winding in night the time   Muslim day
The cross-eyed boy brings dishes.
What's Halima doing in there
Besides cooking?

Greasy rice, warm in the hand.
Pepper flecks on fingers.
Patlican and lamb.

What if you went back there
And thanked her, your bride since ten?
This comes to you, nothing like fear:
You lose another argument with her, in a distant city,
You go to work with her in some sort of factory,
You and cross-eyes over there sit up nights struggling
With another alphabet,
It's not that clear . . .

Go to the door.
Hills are that dull dark, that you love,
Real, near.

Everything is on your lips, once.
You taste it, once.

"LIFE IS VERY STRANGE, AND THERE IS DIYARBAKIR"

(After the film *Yol* by Yilmaz Guney)

So says the man on prison leave,
His hometown reddening, cubic dusk,
Diyarbakir rises from the earth,
Furling laundry at smoke.
He walks more honestly, rubble of walls
Broken over, stooping through gates,
He lifts his legs, children tripping after cigarettes
Clutch at him . . .

Always cities
we knew, knew us.
Their persistence.
Winnipeg, a telephone building,
Stacks of wire synapses, stairs that land half-window,
Archaic, a tower of never mind.
The trapping blue heat of the sky,
Ramp in Ottawa, closed-off,
Weeds crack its jut . . .

"I am listening to Istanbul, intent, my eyes closed."
"In the morning Vancouver's a jewel."
"C'est Paris, il faut pousser."

That man again, crude-hatted,
Diyarbakirli,
Approaching his return, the faces
Silent in the doorways, glimpsed and gone,
The sudden mongrel scrimmages, eyes
Again, reproach and banishment.
The story of away from home.
He stops for water on his face, moves on.
The lane ends. Footsore,
Familiar eloquence of frown and shame.

Still a solidity.
City as final name.

Somewhere they are building it,
Place so alien to you, changes
You, utterly. It is stone
Fitted to stone, a home, the whistle's
Shrillness. The shovels scraping
Barrows, and plaster dust
Stuck to wool. A rising wall.
You watch the builders till they stop, their eyes
That climb you in a finding fear.
You're not from here, and life
Is very strange, and there
Is Diyarbakir.

KOY

And the woman watching us,
our other-worldly bizarreness
curious, stopped this side
that, circling our

car, country we saw her and her people
young and old, come out to cross roads,
waving yellow mushroom strung on sticks
and passed, barely aware of their grouping
the sun hot
Upheld scent of the pines, for us,
sense of an erosive elsewhere . . .

Gunseli saw smoke, and stopped.
A man casually
stood, fanning his hands
behind him, the watery heat from the ditch
flames and forest.

Angered, Gunseli tied on her headscarf
and hobbled towards him, instant crone,
" Please, I was so frightened, my heart
kalbim was pounding, pounding, these beautiful
trees, they will burn up, Effendim."

"Don't worry, mother, nothing will happen."
He politely started to douse it.

Was when his woman watched us, curious
she broke from her skittish goats
and came slowly, a circle
unable to
answer her eyes, ours, the domicile *who?*, to
stop, this side, that, harmless,
touching the bumper, the ridged
headlights, with oh what inner
lit filaments, smiling

into the car. She fled—
Gunseli was back.

"The stupid peasant."

Gunseli gets away now and then
to a guru's western island
and tells him right out You're not God
He won't argue with her
but they cheerfully agree
she'll translate his teachings—
the stumbling block was humility—
Yumushak bashhildi, it is
soft-headed, he's this, that, he does not want
to make a fuss and *alchak* . . .
Well, you call a dog that.

But Gunseli, how we saw her
from the backseat, how she watched us
shy
of our village.

3. :omar

Although I have a handsome face and colour,
Cheek like the tulip, form like the cypress,
It is not clear why the Eternal Painter
Thus tricked me out for the dusty show-booth of earth.

—*The Ruba'iyat of Omar Khayyam*

GOLD SEAL, RAW SILK

Dimaagh, dimaqs, dimaagh, dimaqs,   stamp or seal, raw silk
Donkey-bray at the city's gates, then
The heavens streaming across the sands,
Road to Damascus.
Surfaces lay open in heat to be environments
Of slope and cresciveness, so the eyes said.
Constantly.
I mean to say the goods we handled
Undershone the road, their weight.
How the water sparkled.

I made out :omar from afar, in a
Shimmer, a woman spurring up with him,
Swinging off the saddle hard, with one tug
Setting her horse's head to silence.

We sat on our carpets. :omar was
Civil—for one so often absent I had thought
Talk would be his friend, yet he showed
No interest in the cities, politics
Or any of the gambits that we tried.
Nor did love much interest him.

The woman sat impassively staring into distance.

"Listen," :omar said, "When your tea
Enters the cool tea in your glass, it is
As if its essence has dispersed
In all directions. Don't nod, fool.
The Greeks knew this, the Chinese
And Egyptians. Have some more."

The woman laughed at this. Once.
Then he began to talk.

KHAYYAM   tent-maker

Here I am, at last upon the tide of evening
unfastening my nets to slowly
drag them back and fashion tents
inside tents, corners against stars.
Father stitched a clever pocket for the amir.   prince
My ankles delicately scarred with the old scents,
come carpet, whose ornaments hang in sight's
niches, changing always, like the sides of candles.
Come sleep.
Or in the carpet's level plane feeling the food,
the wine,
seep into me, settle, sand.
What to become? A floor or final resting place for someone
known as me.

On whose surface are plates and bowls suddenly.
I will miss the wine parties,
all that was said and done to me, by me
folded with friends in rooms, and the growing
cold, and finally in the false dawn
outside to stars like these
     and the wheedling pleas
     of bulbuls and babgha'is   nightingales and parrots
                    hyperventilating,
porous, trained perfectly to remember or forget.

One of our company did imitations.
Our cards, tilting on folds of cloth, were prone to
waver underneath, continue, expressing multiples
up or bygone, or the next prime. I might have plucked
a card that wasn't from their fan and scramble
waving pennantly beneath
our knives, our scrapings.

Walking home I would picture al-Hallaj,   tenth-century Sufi mystic
ana al-haqq, I am the truth.   executed for blasphemy;

46

What a claim. Claim or mistaken strategy,   he conveyed an ecstasy
or meaning simply should one take up a discipline,   in which he claimed
one's entitled to make statements.   to be "the Truth."
This they ate up, a choice provocation.
And cheerfully killed *al-haqq*, the truth.
In this sense death is individual, truth
dies in everyone, becomes a floor or final resting place
known as one.

Indivisible

from one who
one night, shaking in his skin
one night will look his last
upon the stars
above Naishapur.

SAND TRACTS

"Poems," said :omar,
With a snide smile, "See
Them make shapes of what is
Subtler, nearly shapeless,
More expansive than the hour before us."

"The winding sand tracts," said the woman.

Evening had been through the several
Blues and lavenders, each revealing
One star, two star, and soon
Our talk was myriad; :omar rocked
On his haunches.
"I wrote a lot of poems when I was young."

The woman excused herself, rode off.
We heard her disappear.

47

"Because I didn't know what else to do with words.
How they were trapped in me and I in them.
How infinitely more honest to listen.
How infinitely small the human voice is.
How will the final sound be as astonished
As the unleashing of all crystal."

Again the woman sat with us.
"I went off," she said. "Nice night."
My companion asked her how she was.
"I sit. I wear my *hejab*. I say little.   head covering
It has nothing to do with you.
Thanks to God, I am well. A ways
From here there is a hollow
Where a breeze is
And a fragrance when one bends to it.
That's where I've been."

"Alif, baa, taa," said :omar, "I had just   first three letters
Conducted a modest nursery tour   of Arabic alphabet
Of my tongue."

But the woman had vanished under her blankets.
"His childhood! Pah!" we heard her say.

THE INFOLDED QUESTION

The whole world collapsed, ingrunting, rubythroated
Coalheap of trouble, glistening, incinerant.

I chilled.

Then saw the world-as-it-was, eerier.
Video-cams, big-screen, satellite, propaganda, distortion, big time.

The girls paraded on the tarmac, filles du macadam,   girls of the road
Led onto the runway for the shah-n-shah,   king-of-kings
Having been raised on country flagstones, fed sweetbreads
                                    and blancmange,
Roquefort and roux, and taught courtesy and charity,
Brought by the planeload to whore for a fete
For Enkidu or Cyrus, yanked
Drugged off the Paris streets by their hair and aching arms
Into the air-bar, taken into jet-lag, Persia.

A closing hand, a folded bird.
They do it again and again, the roiling globe, not to
Break you, but to make you grateful
For your craft, say Iznik tile or Chinese lacquer.
To make you awake to lapis.
To the bark of the arbutus.

Oh, there is pain in you, but none in your living eyes.
Oh don't fold up.

THE HILLS, THE VALLEY

When I say Balkh, deep
In my throat there's a cluster.
Walls that due to tumbling, weather,
Purely human mistakes
Make the mountains only taller, more green.

This city of clearing air kindles
With fires started elsewhere.
Nomads, families huddled in new homes
They strategize and blow on fingers,
Make stew and sip it. The nights are cold,
The stars quaquaversal.

Ka-ash-shilala fawqa-na, a waterfall above us.

So what if your faith isn't mine, our people
Enemies. Who are my people anyway?
They came, like us, to Balkh, to Herat and Kabul
More sorrowful and shorn by their histories than we are.
And more and more come, with their fear,
Their armour of custom and silence:
In short, what we are born to

Not with. Standing on a green hill above Balkh
I might be convinced, if only briefly
That worlds apart, and growing older,
If I sang a simple song and meant it,
You would listen.

*

You would listen, but for years your simple
Act, a passive one, was unbeknownst to me,
Sidereal. They say
Our lives are brief, at once
Bereft and full of ceremony. Ritual
Consumes us, rules, endlessly

We grow older in successive costume,
Neglecting everyday devotions,

Samiira. You were not there in the madrasa   "nightly companion in
To hear me stutter to enunciate   verbal games"/ school
The :arabic alphabet. Though I was certain
At prayer that someone watched me from
The harem, it wasn't you. You missed
My difficult transition; stubborn, blind,
You were the one prayer I could never make,
The fault in my submission.
And I took years to see you, years
To notice how you underlined my words,
Years before I saw your irreal hair,
Ka-al-farasha, butterflies vibrating

The waterfall, and then your irises
Awaken. In spring
The mountains madden, green.
Salaam :alaykum.   peace be upon you

*

Who are my people anyway? And who
Do you place your faith in, Samiira?
The *mujihadiin*, the warring faithful
On their mountain trails, or crammed with their rifles
In a battered Olds? The *muhijratiin*,   the "Petrified," i.e.
                                                those who won't change

Those petrified around their hatreds? A Hindu mob
Surmounting a burning mosque with Soviet weapons?
The dead washed from their fields in Bangladesh
Who flower again in Azerbaijan? Tell me,
Because I suffer, there are no banners,
No tribal scars to part us, and no customs,
Phrases, manners. Tell me the visible
Is superficial.
              Lie to me,
But make it hopeful.

You among women know
The heart has four chambers, two directions
Harb wa Salaam.   war and peace
         Show it to me, burning, secret,
And I'll whisper what I wish:
If it were different. The pledge
We make each instant to the mystery;
My blood has swum out beyond reason
And rebounds to lament our separation—

The most private apartments at such times
Crowd tight around the heart's intention.
Your letters, touched, retraced, released—
The eye's invention.

Daughter of my homeland, if I have one,
It is your condition. Pain,
No way to leave the body. Submission.

Standing in the acrid roar of factories,
Standing on a hill beneath Orion,
Standing at *zawaal* with my hand on the phone,   noon
My heart insists, persists, must tell us where we're from:
A daffodil, a nautilus, a radar dish, the sand:
Ar-raHman.   The Merciful

The winter streets, the bar-signs dark, the women
In the cars, the men outside in tight groups
Smoking . . .

At :eid ul-fiTr, the saris milling, the food, the fond   festival of the fast-
Groups, the men outside in short-sleeves,   breaking
Smoking . . .

They say in the desert between a man and the stars
Is nothing.

In spring the ocean deepens, blue.
Grey-blue.

52

Qadam. to venture, take first step.

Your eyes have listened.

KHOROSAN

Khorosan, coming to it after winters away schooling,
Khorosan. Khayyam's home province
We breathed as we came down the passes, in N.E. Iran
                    wind and wildflowers beside us.
Old walls and new tents.
The thrill was a whole berry
To senses made sensitive
By weeks freezing unasleep by unsympathetic fires,
By sun on the eyes and arms and shoulders in a valley.

"Edge of the petal . . . "
"The skins mashed and a trickle . . . "
"Garden gate . . . "

I was young and thought I could return forever
Like the Qa'ashqa'i tribes, those tattered bands nomadic Iranian tribes
The women squatting and their ululative wails.
But a name is but a habitation;
There is nothing like the curious
bulb of the sun. I have to keep
Telling myself this, because we rise up,
A flame in a form, because we
Gutter, because of time, I have
To keep telling myself . . .

Khorosan. Desert moon. Resemblance.

Shadows so reserved and perverse you keep walking along,
Stateless.

WOMAN OF THE ISLAND

You asked about life in other countries;
For me, that's tourism. We are where we are

Which is most amazing, as a sleep would
Tell us—the unrolling of snow from clouds,

The sun above the ocean at ul-fajr.   dawn, first prayer
And among our favours are the heavens

Exfoliate above us, and the lighthouse and observatory,
And the long lit greenhouses in mist, the Garry oaks.

You asked about the world, sayyida,   lady
And I have seen some of it. The soaring

Domes of Istanbul, and the Manitoba plain
In heavy snow-shine. None has pained

Me like a rainy morning; I rode by; you formed somosa
With your hands, peeled back chapati—

Your head bowed at the stainless sink, the rain—
You left my life. Faaghibti :an hayatii.   You vanished from my life.

Salaam :alaykum, :affa imraata.   Peace, thou chaste woman.
In answer, what's from God, and what is merely human?
May I at least say that, oh island woman?

THE WRITTEN

":omar writes poems about other women,"
The woman said, suddenly, studying
Her hands, then meeting his gaze,
"Because I'm all he's got." She said this
Calmly; it was not a challenge; no, she'd
Thought about the subject, then decided.
"I don't know what to make of it," she added,
"And why bother?"
                        We watched him pretend
Not to respond, which was tedious.
Camped before an unencouraging stretch
Of sand, evening chilling in, the animals
Fed and watered.

"What do you mean, why bother?" :omar said.

"I mean what's the use? So I'm the woman.
I get the here and now, your complaints
When we are travelling, your complaints
Wherever we settle. I get to watch you
Turn and turn again in sleep, and listen
When you wake to all your figmentations—
Some powerfully strange, full of the weirdest
And most fanciful elaborations, so that long ago
 I knew I didn't understand, but understood
You had to make them, and you had to live
A way your voice could shape them. Now
Concerning you my mind is satisfied
Both full and void of questions.

"Yet I know you are not my reflection.
I could comment. I could correct.
But why? I have my own obsessions, regions
Of me in which you merely flicker,
Rider on horizon. My face has been warmed
At other fires, I too have felt a voice
Pull me curious towards it, seen

55

Eyes assess me, known the pointless
Iffing and waffling of selection.
But on I ride! I have admired a bizarre practicality
About your ways, how you refuse
The easy thing to say. If anything
Irks me about those poetic women
They never speak! They lie around,
They bathe, they let the beautiful :ouds   stringed instrument
Caress their ears, their toes revolve
A lotus in a pond, they dine on sweets,
By their fathers they're presented.
Can't you do better than that?"

"No," he said. "I write about them
As of the rare trees of this burgeoning earth,
Birds I've seen, disturbing dreams, no more
Than a serious amusement. I have found
More noble subjects need an apter form
Which is silence. Would I describe the cities
Of Africa I've never seen?; you bet; and here
They are, the huts, the dust, the legs,
The skins, the drums, the armaments.
But what am I writing when of you?
Of what is not completed. If I write
I love you, there's a line
Our eyes have drawn, and drawn again,
And crossed, and this is obvious:
Why then repeat it? If I write
I need you, that is mere hypothesis.
I want you?
You would get tired of it.
The best I could do is write,
I'm with you—
That's already written.
Anyway, you see my problem, or my limit."

"Thank you," she said. "Don't you think
Our companions are sick of this?"

THE PLANET TURAN

Here, said Omar, is a verse about the Planet Turan
Where death came like red dust from the stars
Whose castles and catwalks were fairy-lit
Like nothing in all of the lands.
Warriors in highland costume waged
Merciless slingsword massacre on small birds.
There were divers at all depths,
Spies with their own publications,
Surveillance, everywhere surveillance,
Until Turan proclaimed itself the paranoic
Capital of the known universe.
Intensely aware of their own modesty
And the thirteen ways to meet a princess,
The Turanish preened in their many-levelled apartments,
Silkily giving onto the stars odours of ozone
And perfume and shoulderblades.
At their exclusive parties
Over the harbours, in the green highlands
Theirs was ribald talk of life in the Zones.

They lay to the West
Where the sky was sooted over
And the earth like a meteor.
Weird light playing over factory tin-walls,
Roads smashed, new trails over chalky marshes,
Spontaneous looting and murder. A band
Of Turanish gentlemen were held
For years in a flooded basement, played
Tapes of classical maqaam and MOR Turanish   tonality, mode in music;
Muzak, allowed to breathe   a type of musical progression
With swimming rats, mutated rats, nibblers,   of variations
Parasites. Played tapes of game shows,
Tapes of surgical procedures, taken for
Long walks in the middle of the night
To abandoned elementary schools,
Talked to patiently in miniature classrooms.
At the harbour parties it was common knowledge

The gents had been on a sex tour.
And the laughter drifted up
Like smoke.

That is what Turan came to, the dead,
The jewelled, the splendid ladies in sparkling train,
The jugglers and their gliding vehicles,
The machines for ascent and descent,
The changing mirror, the profound
Peace of carpets or of stately ponds,
The library of a lit tree—What holds,
What passes, evanescent.

Morning your eyes met the sky.
Jawan.   intense passion

THE SHELL

The dust on the horizon, west, east,
The Ti'en Shan, the spelling of hooves   "The Mountains of
Spelling what but incessance, and boundaries . . .   Heaven"
World pain, then, as it is said
The Seljuks come out of Asia,   11th c. Turkmeni con-
Bringing their bad habits with them.   querors of Persia
Their cruelty, their love of plunder and amassment.
It is like they are our weather, beyond us.
Later today, the swelling sunken banks of gold
     in spectral traces.
This too distributed.

Three thousand years from the Iranian plateau
Caught in queues of various duration
Others may remember how
The Sassanians came, and before them Sumer
And before them the folk of Uruk, came   *Gilgamesh's* "walled
With their signs and their shapes of   city of Uruk"
God and animals while the stars retraced
Their beautiful elapsement.
Left to those ends, the stars would be but lonely
So we spread out spiralled like a birthing necklace
As coral keeps an island, as divers
Burst from the foam with bulging eyes

Take air, remember
How the mudhdhan climbed into the dawn   prayer-caller
Helixed, reglimpsed, eclipsed,
Winding, a candle in the cold.
Samarra. Oh, Samiira   the beautiful winding-
Edge of my ear, I tell you   staired minaret in Iraq
      there is laundry drying in Northern Paris,
There are sheets drying and sand
Beaches in Thailand, in Malaysia, and tents in the ground
And safety and your people
And the skies.
       And the shape of an eight.

And the horizon.

So the Seljuks come for us
Intent on robbing something essential
Our souls perhaps.
A wonder we'd worry; tell another
You've a soul, prepare to lose it.
Give up, send delegates.

:omar, your mother warned you, you
Would hand your brother to them
For another night of pleasure
And revel in edges, desert,
Passing through towns as though they offended you,
Man of no fortune, with a name to come

Among us, mirror and contempt, a shivering glint
Alongside the lacustrine cities,
Dwellers in glass caves, the numbering, the luminous
People we've seen before, nowhere in particular—
Other cities, perhaps—Or at the farthest
Extremity of families. Relation is
No simple thing, and neither is identity.
Kaan wa ma kaan.   There was and there wasn't.

Umm al-lu'ulu'u , there are young men slinging sitars   mother-of-pearl
              on raised platforms in the Scythian lands.
And young women with their hair fluorescent
                    and their nostrils jewelled, right here.
There are sails and whitecaps all over the earth.
The polar star.

Raincloud, say the Seljuks came for us, all right.
Wonder is they took so long.
We were ready for our unexpected meeting.

60

RIHLA   journey

We woke to :omar and his companion,
Huddled, talking late, till the dawn fire,
Talking low and secretively:

"Tomorrow we reach Damascus,
There will be your mathematical klatches,
Circles of talk and bragging and
Lying about wisdom."
"I know," he said,
"Tomorrow the city,
For you will be the company of women,
Admiration and silks and bracelets
And the beauty of the young."
"Not if I can help it,"
She said. "I like to get away and keep
The horses company, think about things.
Their smell, their simple, big-eyed need
Of what is human. And they love the wind."

"I wonder if they, too, have incomplete
Ideas and torture reason in their name?"
Said :omar. Then he sighed. "Look, Samiira,
Have I hurt you, much?"
"Look in my eyes,

Man of no fortune, do you witness
Any of the past in them, its pain?"
"I can't," he said. "And you?
Lover of the bright world, can you
Find in my face the future?"
"I can't," she said. Then sighed.

"So let us rest on that."

"Still, I could tell you things . . . "
Said :omar, through a yawn. She
Chuckled, drew him to her. "Tomorrow,

Witless, we have got to bargain hard
For proper saddles . . . "

4. Hurriya

What can a flame remember? If it remembers a little less than is necessary, it goes out; if it remembers a little more than is necessary, it goes out. If only it could teach us, while it burns, to remember correctly.

GEORGE SEFERIS

If only there were occasion for repose
If only this long road had an end
And in the track of a hundred thousand years, out of the heart of dust,
Hope sprang again, like greenness.

—*The Rubaiyat of Omar Khayyam*

THE BALANCE

"He left," the boy said, awake
To the enclosing canvas.
"Of course. It was obvious he would.
And for all his talk I am no wiser."
He rolled over, but could not dispel
The thought; it drove him to a crouch
In the dark. He gathered himself
In his father's even breathing.

He laughed.

"What did I expect? At least
He has not diminished me.
I wanted someone who would
Recognize my best and not let
Me drift into imitation.
Not let me be other than I am."

The boy touched his face,
His chest, his legs, then saw a figure
Traversing the void, his eyes
Fixed downwards, intent on each step.
Too intent.
                    "But what of him?
Has he diminished himself? When I saw
Him riding up, days ago, that face—
It held magic, wisdom, patience, truth.
Little by little the road stripped these
From him." The boy thought. "You know,
I never heard him laugh. Always with him
Was that stress I've seen with my father.
He lives life a long ways out in front of him,
And busy, has to keep busy, like :omar
Has to talk. There is nothing in the present
Holding him; everything is part of the eventual.
But no, that is not it."

He thought for a long time.

When his father woke he studied his face.
Then went to see Samiira. She met
His footsteps with exaggerated readiness.

"Have you come to see the master?
Our famous poet? He is no longer here.
What was your first clue? His manner
Of speech? Sort of a cross between
Oration and delirium. His eyes?
Focussed merely on what his mouth spun.
Or his alternation of lullaby
And insulting condescension?"

He looked at the ground.

"I have heard your words," he said,
"But their rhythm knocks against their sense.
I have heard your sadness.
Listen: what's for you won't go past you."
She glared at him.
"Perhaps what's for me is its passing,"
She replied.

The boy took a long time gathering
And securing their things. His father
Watching. Finally the boy let
A samovar drop in the sand, stood there
Blankly looking at it. The man put a hand
To his shoulder. "My son, don't waste
Your sadness. He is he; you are another.
A man not tied by his heart
To others has nothing to do
But wander.
Go forth and earn your sorrow."

"But what was he trying to tell us?"
Urged the boy. "What was it all about—

Those poems, places I've never heard of,
names summoning nothing, like dire
Confrontations with ghosts. The woman
Thinks he was insulting us."

"Did you feel insulted?"
"No." "Well?"
They strapped bags to the animals.
"I think he was telling us something, that's all."
"Oh, I think so too. I've never heard him talk
Like that before. I strained to hear
A distant merriment in there, until I realized
I was listening for the past. I think
He tried to tell us he lost his balance."

"He didn't try very hard, then. I would
Have sworn he thought he had the answers."

" Listen, the world is large, bewildering, by turns
Beautiful , sickeningly ugly. The mind must
Enter it and move. If all dimensions flood
The mind at once. . ." His father shook his head.
"He had the questions."

THE MIDNIGHT PAVILIONS

And :omar stood rocking with
A replicative wave and a single star,
O rough glint sticking in the trough,
Facing Port Angeles—by day
Smuggy, lost in the grey ocean
Eaten by Olympic peaks.
But now how bright and close.
His tears freezing, his feet
Fixed.
Midnight, his shape in the open pavilion.

How could he not love
His own time, or feel lost in it,
Alien
          Man of no fortune, with a name to come.
How not recognize his own people
Since their image, unrestrained
By belief beyond their images
Was the language :omar breathed, and saw
Coded in the patterns of clothes, the hair
Adorned, braided or layered, the games
Played by the children on the lawns,
Attack, divide and whelm, division of limbs,
Ministers rising to make sentences and similar,
The hackysacks spinning from their feet, the garish
Plastic guns, the swords—and all the multiple
Obsessions of the tribe flickering on computer screens,
Charts of gain and mayhem, or mutating
Webs, or depth fields signalling space
Collapsed in him to a tree-filled carpet.
What then was in earnest, what the real?
Speech came from their mouths, bewildered him.
As he had noticed his did them.

But, no, that was not it.
:omar stood rocking in the wave
Of the star. He could not go

Beyond his single thought:
Abandon.

In the pavilion nightly a party
Of loud drunk voices wound around him.
The tables heavy with meats and cheeses,
Empanadas, dipping veggies. The world's endless
Variety of liquid in bottles. He had spoken

With a woman who did not know the language
Very well, he could tell because when jokes
Were told, she didn't always laugh, or did
Too late. Do you understand, he asked?
Oh yes. You didn't laugh. And her look
Was hurt, lost, but she smiled.
When alone what place did she dream of?

But that was not it.

Abandon.

The party took place on a staircase
Lightly iced. People drifted there to smoke,
To talk of plans. Was it the moment
When he was asked, Are you with this lady?
(No.) Was it when another woman said
You should stay, and he left? (No.)
Was it his friend, huge, pissed,
Lumbering towards those stairs
That may or may not have supported him?
(He was intercepted.)

Was it the same people gathered
Before his friend, big-hearted, huge
In his enthusiasms, flat on his back,
Dead, not much later.

How people talk and talk around
the one thing they will not say.

How the wave chops and rocks.
The star, floating.

THE CITIES

And lost interest in cities, :omar said:
They mislaid me. Who were they
To ignore my uprightness, O little fig,
Salaaming twig,
Holding my hopes up with tiny hands,
Head up with flattened feet.
Indifference: the clouds effaced
In glass, and towers to drink the sun
In phlegmy strings, all those mouths in hierarchy,
Their virtue in afforded space;
My shame a simple body
In the streets, too visible, insane, insane,
The mouths insisted, look at it speak, the sickened
Fool. Another brain to feed.

No, they never had need of me.
They had a vertical arrangement on the plain,
The neatest gardens and the firmest locks,
The use of vehicles, their inbred heavens.
Useless the mouth I honed
On the finest words, the lips I'd soften
For your hearing ear, the heart
Enlarged against a continent. My speech
A midden from them, vulgarists.
The strange stamp of my face.
Or so I weakened.

You know, Samiira, I sang to them as they passed.
My heart sang in me that I was of their family.
How ardently I tried to please

Myself, to sing better and better of a fearsome
Unity I dreamed. A foetus
Curled against the spine, and rocking, rocking
In the warmest of harbours, eerie its glass ears,
Its brightened, gentle eyes: can this suffice
As picture of that love?
A thudding of bloods
Began to deafen me.

I raged.
My voice's resin clotted, choked me.
I rasped.

Was lonely.

My skin sweated, ached in my clothes, and
My mind became like wafer—the winter day-moon.
Chattering legs swarmed around my shape.
The city grew. Soon, in gruesome pattern
The metal rooves boned out the sky, and the people
Narrowed at the eyes, became a species
Crowding my hollow joints, furiously
Discussing stolen laundry, the city
Limp with stinging smoke, humped and spired
To the sea, and I heard inside
Their strange worship of the number three
And their clankety ratchet: Do this, Do that.
How they strangled in the whitest cloaks their fear.
And would not talk to or look at each other.
The city resembled their souls, and was recorded.

Thirsty, feverish, for a long time
In their offices and drinking holes I overheard
And spat out their flattened voices.
I dreamed of terminals, of footsteps and incandescent platforms.
My name became the frailest set of ladders.
Knives grew from my toes, from which I fashioned
Severe mathematics for the dust to question.
Newspapers blew against me, and fine gold wrappings.

71

Candles pushed through my forehead, leaving furrows.
I snapped these off and tried to hide them.

My skulk finished, I stood up, became a city
Able enough after centuries to shelter.
Fragranced by new songs,
Children on my awkward corners,
Lovers sunning in my fairest places.
Why, I asked my heart?
Samiira, it did not answer
Vagabond, I sing only that this is possible.

THE TAVERN

And the words stopped
and the visions stopped
the words :omar had so little trouble linking
taking part of a shiny coy one
from this language
reconfiguring it in that
a boldly moving word
until he beheld reality
plain, swimming into its mystic depths
holding a word by the tail or the mouth
and the lights stopped—
purple and yellow scimitars
—and the song stopped
his throat no longer vibrated nor
did his chest swim with exhalted dizziness
in the clear winter air
above the bridged city
calling to the sleepers from his
throttled heart
and his constant walking stopped
his pleasure in the offhand

conversation with a chance companion and
the currency of female eyes met
in the street or tavern that refilling thrill
stopped
He dragged himself from the harbour
on a rainy night and asked
Who am I?

Laughter from a band of souls
and a few dogs around a small fire
What place is there in the world for me?
His shoes wet, his skin damp and cold
:omar saw the tavern door glowing
feeling in his beard younger, confused
The proliferation of windows way up
the moving sounds in the water
What was it all about, that dream?
There was a boy, and a woman
I knew them, but they kept changing roles.
I knew him, but when he was least
Like me. Such a void between us.
The ache of all he'd do—and all
I'd never want. Then her.

:omar stumbled over three lanes
and the winter sidewalk into the tavern.
And sat, plainly thinking.
"What was I thinking of then?
Of knowing others—but there—
in the desert—When they rode upon me—
Cloaken—You could see in their
Hard, cruel faces that it wasn't mutual.
And her—well, she was sorry for herself.
Enough said—Or no—It comes
Before my eyelids—Her pleasure sated
With the robbers, content with their plunder.
Her due. —Or that she will always forgive
Herself, change nothing.
                    That is a painting

I have made. My distance, my suspicion.
It is the boy I need.
                            How I hid behind him
Mocking his earnest questions. And yet
With him before me, how I spoke the truth,
My truth. Gave him my best poems.

"Can I get you something, sir?"
She'd been standing at his table some time.
"I need the boy."
                            She stepped to one side, studied him.
"Pardon?"
            "Forget the woman, it's the boy I need."
"I'm not sure what to advise. I meant to drink."
"Wine! Before life's liquor in its cup be dry!"
("Smashed already," she reported to the barkeep.
"Aw, he's always here; is he on about the boy again?"
"There's a woman involved, too."
"Oh, there's a woman involved, is there?")

Before long :omar was on the street again.

HURRIYA

Freedom, ah freedom.
And who will explain to you what freedom is?
And what will form a picture of this?
Or are you queered to it already,
Told to by the rumbling of the rancid radio
Cowboys and their argot in the brain
Policemen detailing their experience
Religious groups vying for your piety—
Who would have thought there'd be a competition,
So many mumblers pleading for your liberation.
But it is not this, nor any imitation
Nor studied habit, nor proud association.
Look at us, a continent
Completely free to build a pastel condominium
With a pittance of cedar bark for Nature;
Unleashed to slander and demean in any number
Of bars resembling British locals.
Is this what we mean by Hurriya?
By "knife in heart" the Chinese mean
To present "tolerance."
And "truth" a man standing beside his word,
And "man" a strong figure beside ordered fields.
How are we queered to it, our freedom, stunned from birth
Climbing and climbing a nest of symbols.
And those who fall out of the shaped rejectumenta, nest:
Insane, abject, the non-included—
The poet peers into this heart, forgets his language,
And finds his breath, "the jewel," against his ribcage.
The Turkish boy who laughed, let go his father's hand
And ran beside the sea to kiss his neighbour, little girl,
Shocked to a quick giggle at him.
Freedom they will lose at adolescence.
The labourers leave off and fill the tarred boat
With fresh narcissi. In Bangladesh
The madman roams the brilliant fields
With his songs and instrument, pollen-eyed,
His feet bare. On our own streets

The humour of the destitute, the mimers and the chanters
Please us more than festivals, than regulated Santas.
It is not that it is useless to play the crowd,
Or steer a ferry. It is that our ideas
Of ourselves are too serré.
It is not that the world is harsh, devoid of pleasure,
It is our eyes fixed always on a bankrupt measure.

Or that we have lived so long with our sickness
That we lust after words, their sleek reflections
Words that sate and smother sight—"white trash,"
"A flake," "the sinner."
There is courage to see again, and there are cringers.
What are the well-dressed people carrying in their cameras
After all but expectations. And us. And we
Who would sell our water and wood to them,
Would make their beds and twist our names and history
For them have come together, crowded,
Hungry for smutty cartoons and boring video
Of police at work, hungry for garments, jewels,
Irreally sprayed and fattened food.
Hungry for identity: subjection.

O the roar of the crowd singing of kings.
O the roar of the crowd
Is as lonely as anything.

Is freedom then rejection of one's own culture, finally,
A rejuvenation? Is it to manage a local economy
To the point of opening new resorts, yet maintaining
A moral foothold away from "the masses"?
To home schoolchildren until they feel superior?
Is it pride in one's own path?
A taste for inner luxury?
Or to wrest love from the familiar, and proclaim
No figment of the earth as alien. Our strangest
Dreams and needs tend to unity; but these have strangely
Ogred into war, and grim calamity.

:omar lifted his hand from the table,
Reconsidering.
                  The dream of unity,
Of freedom in the heart, why is it
That to preserve this, one turns from
The inevitable clash of armour,
From the toppling nations,
From the shifting maps, to find
What? A holy loneliness.
The world cannot be hid from,
Nor can the penetrating thought
That comes in the night
That comes with the frost
That the outcomes are beyond you,
The dream of unity one
You'll never wake to:
What you can hope for only
Is that the dream outlives you.
That change not wholly silt around you
So you see the rushing river
From the bed bottom, the sun
Beyond a moving barrier...dream-white,
Blurred . . . aethereal. . .

:omar let the thought die
But no, he couldn't leave it there:

So what was I thinking of—
I had in mind a world of
Utter spontaniety, flamboyant
Acts of passion, kindness,
Individualized celebrity.
A world full of brilliant talk
And madcap lovers—and this vision
Led me, fed me, kept me up at night
And all day running and running
Down what rose in my body
What slashed from my mouth.
Easy to criticize, to mock the surface.

But always in my fevered haste
Was something missing.
At first I thought it was the city's fault;
Our place gives us a portion
Of itself to hand along—a face, a currency.
Second, I thought it was my enemies.
But they were only what I made them.
Then I remembered a couple of patient
Voices, who tried to speak to me:
":omar, if someone else has a problem,
You don't have to get involved."
And: "To find happiness,
Beneath the busy fabric of life,
One makes careful choices."

I saw I had no idea
What they meant.
I lunged, I fled.

Samiira rose and gently pushed him back in his chair.

THE VALLEY, THE HILLS

My eyes have listened, and my soul
Is troubled too. I have stood
Behind the waterfall, in calming damp
And let my ears fill with the inevitable
Rush, the roar, the incoming mist.
How different the world seemed through that veil!
The green outside, blurred through diving flashes;
Looming, fresh, mysterious. A spider
Web and its precise inhabitant.
The cool, rough walls of the cave, formed
In the only way possible for a cave
To form, behind a waterfall, in this place.

Sat outside on a rock, let the sun
Take weight from my hair, talk to my skin.

Do you know postcards, :omar? Generally they offer
A relaxing, sunny place, an invitation
To join a friend, to share that thing
Called happiness. I have seen other cards.
The bedraggled families in makeshift
Tents, boys with beautiful eyes:
Men by virtue of their weapons, held
Up, casually leaned on, thin chests
Filled out by bandoliers, jungle-clipped
Ammunition. Men hauling a rocket-
Launcher up a hill. Tanks. The message
Is the connection: Wish you were here
To join our struggle.

That will end when the war is over.
But it is never over, and the goal gets lost.
The cards and their angry slogans circulate.
General truths fixed to small purposes
Shade into lies. It is said there is a winner
In such things, and so the loser plans, hurt,
To win in the future, get something back.

79

We live in tribes, and shout (to ourselves)
We're strong! But never strong enough,
I fear, to stop.

Meanwhile the earth
Tolerates us. Though whole crops are lost,
And rivers silt up, and the oceans blacken,
And the sky absorbs our burning dwellings,
And what we dispose of lies deep
Within the earth, leaching its slow poison,
And villages are abandoned, and species
Dwindle, and whole peoples drift across
The map, crowded in airports; though families
Are separated, the men roaming farther
And farther in search of money; though young
Women are sold into the sex trade;
Machines talk faster and faster to each other
About profit, loss, contingency and risk—
The seasons continue gently to astonish us.
Each night the sky dulls and deepens.

It is what the body needs, this pattern.
And the heart? It cannot be kept
Wholly clear of the world's confusion,
Because it knows what it knows, and the eyes
Have seen what they have seen.

They have seen the smoke rise
From the valley to the hills,
And rain slant through it incessantly.
And birds scatter and form purposeful clouds.
And blinked at lightning.
Scanned words and pictures.
And they have met other eyes, if only briefly
And listened.

This is why I come and breathe
Cool earth behind this veil of water.

*

What if the veil fell?
What if there were nothing
To separate me and you, or anybody
No borders to cross with documents
No stories to retell in our own favour,
No reason to keep silent, and no
Words to keep from children.
Gone the empires, gone the crowds of oil
Of cigarettes passing the blockbuster movie billboards.
The map-fantasies, gone, the misleading texts,
Gone the tendrillous, nerve-clutching gases.
Would it then be possible to see people for their worth
And not their usefulness?

Would there not still be this insufferable romance
Of you calling to me in various guises?
We all make bargains with reality —
We may know what we hate, and pay
The price of avoidance; holding to that
We don't know if the terms have changed.
Yet we are safe.

The eyes have seen what they have seen,
My ribcage listened.
Have, the implosive crunch of cat-treads over aluminum walls and
rooves,
Have, the shadows drifting to their spots on corners after curfew,
Have, the crowd rise, one, immense, howling.

Who are my people? In truth
They are less inclusive than you'd like:
They cleaned airports for twenty years so I could grow up
Relatively sheltered.
They struck deals with men who despised them.
They sang me songs in our language long, long after the shouting
faded,
While the burning continued, so I could sleep.

They told all manner of lies to ensure my safety.
They calmed me and made me laugh when the other children
Called my name "silly" or "weird."

And millions more have stooped
And stolen, left everything, their limbs
Raked by wind, telling themselves
Just one step forward, one more, you
Can do it for your family, forget your equally
Frightened connections in the government,
Your livelihood, leave under cover of dark
Ride with strangers for days without food—
The bitterness of places you once thought
It would be interesting to pass through!—
As they hushed the children's tears
Those sobs conformed to their unvoiced ones' shapes
And they entered the silence
Loss is, one does not speak of—

And you wonder that such people, newly homed
Suddenly skilled at impossible decisions
Should have faith in customs.
Or having moved so far, once, in fear, in haste
Should think one strange who moves on,
Moves on, moves on. If the wind be pleasure,
You are gone.

To accept in the bones a life in part sustained
By something missing? To change
In careful increments, dulling the risk, the pain.
To grow old in the same way as your parents. . .
I may as well lecture you about the moon.
She's infinitely accessible, a better listener, comely, too,
Remote, therefore desireable.

Man of no fortune,
I cannot speak to you of this without
Distortion; what each of us
Has been denied, eludes:

This is our portion.

This is why I come and breathe cool earth
With a spider, behind a veil of water.

SUSTAINABLE

I came into the world, :omar said
Not to fill a need in it, but
To capture and inhabit a time
For myself. I came to unfold
From my heart, to find words
Praising creation. What do I care
That the centuries press around us,
That they summon us to debt, to sorrow
Passed from chest to chest? A mutual
Misery is not love. Yet if I could
Help you, I would help you. If knew
You, I would have reached the goal:
To know myself. I mean my soul.

But how curious I am, we are, about
Inessentials. We want to be given
What will paint our natures on our eyes.
Want to know what we cannot—
Why what is, is.
                    In the streets
The young shout dire warnings,
Or crouch on sidewalks and ask for change.
"I'm too poor to know anything," one told me.
"What was it all about anyway?" an old man said.
"Thank you trees for the nice day," my daughter said,
Her face a small light.
                    Who then has wisdom?

Not me: I came to praise
The banners of what-have-you,
Ephemeral display our minds are daily
Dipped in, drying, notion, inclination.
I came to say our languages
And signs, the foods we make, the traffic
Of our actions, our wars and misconceptions,
Our customs changing always, our fabulous
Dress, the chemistry of births and marriage
Night and day and night again
Sustain us.
            Samiira snorted.
There's that word again. :omar is
Too much of his time. All the pain
In the world has taught him little if
He sees in our foul-smelling panoply,
Our barking languages abutted to each
Other, mocking, talking down to those
We scarcely know, our not-too-subtle
Marks and emblems of assumed superiority—
Which includes our faddish repetition
Of "recycle," "act locally," "pro-active"
And so forth—if in this, and our profound
Tendency to drop everything and wallow
At the sound of money changing hands,
He sees in all this a comforting magic,
Enough to carry the whole rainbow-laden planet
Into futures. . .

Is that what he meant? said the boy,
(For :omar had wandered over to the windows),
Or did he mean by "us," the sustainable,
A human need to save something personal
From the fray, to hold to love, or image
Of love as a stay against confusion;
Else enter the whirlpool, aflail at that
Which none controls, bitter, crushed
By the inescapable tragedy of being one?

A mutual misery is not love, said Samiira,
He got that part right.
                    You loved him,
What was that like? the boy asked.

Like snowfall, she said,
And would not continue.

THE BOY

Stood, then, in the tavern,
Dismissing :omar's sarcastic grin,
Samiira's worried smile, stood
And one, two, mounted the table,
Surveying them, surveying all, the fans
Turning in the voices, the bright
Panels of disparate art on the walls, barmaids
In their expensive ankle-length dresses.
:omar fell silent. Samiira
Stared impassively into distance.

Then he began to talk:

Plainly a great deal is expected
Of human beings these days,
I mean we gotta be conscious
Of who did what to whom and who's
Still owed and even our sex
Is gravely suspect—I mean
What'd I do to "the goddess"?
And not only the competing
cultural values as we hitchhike
for $7 an hour along the information highway

85

it's the national debt I have or
don't have in my pockets
I must have a short, medium
and long-term strategy for the rent
my "career-track" and "mating-
window"—did I make that up
or overhear it?—anyway
I can't make up my mind
which is dangerous between
Bosnian solutions, James Joyce's relevance
and alternatives to clearcutting
I suppose I'll have to educate
myself until I'm overqualified
all these problematic thoughts
under my hairnet
"Do you want fries with that?"
And so I say fuck it
And so I say if I sang a simple song
you'd probably laugh at me.
                                    You think
too much. I mean here we are,
We get up, we work a bit, we go out
And laugh and what the hell. Yet
Here you sit debating the justice
Of the universe—:omar's impossible
Ideals and Samiira's tortured loyalties.
Shit. In the caravan, you know
At least we were getting somewhere—
You guys go around and round yet
Tell—have you really changed?

And don't hit me with some rigmarole
About your "spiritual growth" or your
"commitment." You're torturing each other
With what you think you could be,
Respectively. But, like, if only it were respectfully.
How about what you are?

Now I will make plain what I mean—

I've been watching you two, and because
Of my deep respect for you I'm going to
Disregard completely what you've been saying—
In fact, I'm going to tell you a thing or two.
See this—he pointed to his head—
And this—his heart. Let me whisper
In your ears. When these two are in line
That is freedom, which isn't staying away
From the general melee, and isn't trying
To argue people into your little circle.
What is it? I'll give you an idea.
I rolled out of bed this morning
Onto a little cloud, sooty below and
Gilded above, and drifted over the city,
Then watched the counterweight
Take the blue bridge up and cars and cars
And buses and to the north a
Delicious rainbow opened my mouth
To the toqued and baggy-assed skateboarders.
Zoop, zoop their spin and clatter at the ramp-
Lip! I had several interesting chats
With beggars. I watched a screen and made
Entries on the screen so I could afford
A hell of a good falafel with hot sauce
At lunch in a place with pretty waitresses—
So shoot me! Oh, and some weird guy with
Ruffles around his neck handed me a poem,
Which I read, and took in his rap
About "the mind" and "art." How
Quaint or dumb the cooks on break
Look smoking cigs with puffy hats.
In the late p.m. I came upon
A man who'd hit his head, a woman
Knelt by his ear, "I won't leave you
Till they come to take care of you."
All right, and with my other eye
The crane in the sky, a tiny man
Up there, placing huge weights,
Drawing necks back at his performance.

And balancing bike couriers.

                          And the sidewalks dark

In winter.

              And the way wind pushes the

Sun's shape across a finer

                    Ripple in the inlet.

People dressed up as trees

                      Before the legislature.

So much happened and I saw

So little I could do to change it

I decided to be myself.

That's what the planet

Seems to want from me.

That's all. Bye now. Our

Revels now are ended—

                    check it out.

And he left.

SAMIIRA

You say it's inevitable we be together
I say turn your back on me once, at least
Permit me the enjoyment of a similar reflex.
I say in our conversation there has been static
Migraine, crossed signals, white noise, interference
And I need to make contact with a deep silence.
Your talk goes around and around not forward—
That perhaps is your genius, to spin
Traumatically, sucking in the sound bites
Of the planet. I make choices, step towards them,
Close the door, never look back.
Not for a good long while. Though the sexes
Are made differently, I don't think that explains
The distance I contemplate you from, after our journey
After our long and hectic struggle with tolerance.
Man of no fortune, believe me, you have not been betrayed:
You've been rejected.

And she left.

THE TRUTH

It became evident in the susurrus and swill sound
Of which he heard only women's voices
He didn't know it.
Not even.
Of it X-vested workers picking pylons from a long line, back of a
                                                              truck,
Of it a desolate landing-pad of cracked asphalt in the morning amid
    broken furniture, mattresses wet and swollen, shards of bottles,
    and long, long strands of cassette tape, surrounded,
Of it the young cross-legged in building-entrances, heads bent, folded
    under sleeping bags, "Any change, Sir?"
Of it Samiira's changing eyes,
Of it the weather,
Of it a baby's first smiles at a caterpillar-face, a rubber toy,
Of it a Haida figure's ferocious carved grin and its hands up,
    surrendered.
Those who wanted to talk to him
Of their lostness and anger and driftwood;
Those who didn't want to talk to him
Of his anger and lostness and personal references;
Those who were indifferent.
Of it fit together, how, :omar ruefully didn't know.

:omar had watched the faces pass downtown
As though they contained a great secret;
In the mirror at home his own face
Looked about the same. Human.

His father's snarling
His lashing, to restrain
The unexceptional rebellions of a moody boy,
His mother's lies, to erect
Guilts around him, a disconnected
Phone booth.

These were not the truth, whole.
Nor small pills he took into his body

For fear, for doing things in order,
The extravagant apologies he made
And unmade, a rucked-up bed . . .

:omar let it fall from him, rise in him, fall . . .
The trees of Vancouver had not such transience,
Their delicate pink blossoms, pink-white, gone.
The planet-wandering barks and branches,
Seeds and the skein of various winds:
Spring wind, tiptoe wind, face-forward wind,
Shoulder-stiff wind,
Nostalgic winter wind, Winnipeg
Buildings shorn from the sidewalk.

The solemn ring of female faces stared
From a collapsed home in Herat . . .

Someone tossed a stir-stick at a giggling table . . .

I was . . .they did. . . we were. . . this meant . . .
He ruefully couldn't . . .

Even though there should be
A small reasonable saying he could trade
For explanation
For the careful consolation
Of being human
And what to do next
With his head unfilled by approximate truths
And a small distaste for answers
In his pen
:omar sat blinking in the tavern.

"Last call?"
"Coffee. . ."

Acknowledgement

Thanks to the editors of the following journals and programmes who published or broadcast parts of *Hurriya*: *arc*, *The Malahat Review*, *Prism International*, *CBC State of the Arts*, *The Toronto Review of Contemporary Writing Abroad*.

Many people contributed to these poems: thank you. I would particularly like to mention Lee Gowan, Susan Gillis, Susan Donaldson, John Orser, Erin Moure, Al Purdy, Patrick Lane and Jay Ruzesky who read the manuscript in whole or part and offered their comments over the years.

The author gratefully acknowledges the financial assistance of the Canada Council and the British Columbia Cultural Services Branch.

The quote on p. 15 is from *The Country North of Belleville* by Al Purdy; "Who Is to Match You . . . " on p. 17 is adapted from Tabbat Ash-sharran; italics on p. 18 from The Guess Who's "Running Back to Saskatoon"; "Man of No Fortune . . ." on p. 60 is from Pound's *Cantos*.